Nice Shot!

(And Other Lies Golfers Tell Each Other)

A Golfer's Guide to Lies, Trash Talk and Excuses
(A Funny Golf Gift)

Ricky Woods

Copyright © 2025 Ricky Woods

Published by: Bemberton Ltd

All rights reserved. No part of this book or any portion thereof may be reproduced in any form by any electronic or mechanical means, without permission in writing from the publisher, except for the use of brief quotes in a book review.

The publisher accepts no legal responsibility for any action taken by the reader, including but not limited to financial losses or damages, both directly or indirectly incurred as a result of the content in this book.

ISBN: 978-1-915833-81-5

Disclaimer: The information in this book is general and designed to be for information only. While every effort has been made to ensure it is wholly accurate and complete, it is for general information only. It is not intended, nor should it be taken as, professional advice. The author gives no warranties or undertakings whatsoever concerning the content. The reader accepts that the author is not responsible for any action, including but not limited to losses, both directly or indirectly incurred by the reader as a result of the content in this book.

View all our books at **bemberton.com**

CONTENTS

5   Introduction: The Fine Art of Golf BS

11   On the Tee — Where Hope Dies Quickly

25   On the Fairway (Or More Likely, the Rough)

39   Short Game — Chunks, Blades, & Total Meltdowns

55   Bunker Banter — Excuses from the Sand

71   The Green — The Land of Broken Dreams

87   The 18th Hole — When the Wheels Come Off

101   The Clubhouse — Where Everyone is a Hero

113   Conclusion: See You Next Round

INTRODUCTION:
THE FINE ART OF GOLF BS

Golf is a game of lies.

Some are subtle and hard to detect. Others are right in your face. Either way, lies are everywhere on the course.

This book is here to translate them into language you can actually understand. It won't always be pretty, or pleasant, or nice to hear — but it will be honest.

In the pages that follow, we'll wander through the course — just like you do most Saturdays, chasing one sh***y drive after another. Only this time, you'll get the hard truth about the game — and your place in it. We're not sugarcoating anything.

There's no promise you'll feel better about your game by the end of this book.

You won't. You'll feel worse.

And that's fine.

Because there's a strange kind of freedom in seeing the truth for what it is:

This is a dumb game.

You suck at it.

And the sooner you accept that, the sooner you might actually enjoy this ridiculous hobby.

Wait—did we say enjoy?

Never mind. That's not happening.

WHY GOLFERS NEVER SPEAK THE TRUTH

On the surface, golf is a friendly, gentlemanly sport. People dress nicely. They speak politely. They follow a long list of etiquette rules to keep things civil. Trash talk might be common in other sports—but not here.

So, does that mean golfers like and respect each other?

Not even close.

Just because golf isn't full of in-your-face trash talk like other sports doesn't mean the sh*t talk isn't happening. It's just... disguised. Hidden under layers of forced smiles, subtle jabs, and loaded encouragement.

Try speaking the truth on the course—really saying what you think—and you'll quickly find yourself playing alone. Honesty doesn't belong here. So instead, the game is built on lies and half-truths. From the outside, it all looks peaceful.

Friendly. Harmonious.

But regular golfers know better.

A CULTURE OF FAKE ENCOURAGEMENT

Ever noticed how golfers always seem to root for each other?

You've heard the lines:

"Go ahead, knock this one in."
"Hit it close."
"Good luck, play well."

Why are golfers always being so damn nice to the people they're trying to beat?

Here's the truth: they're not.

Golf has created a weird little culture of fake encouragement — where we say polite things we absolutely do not mean. Over and over. With a straight face.

Do you really want your opponent to split the fairway?

Of course not. You want him to slice it into the tree, bounce backward, and end up in a pond next to an angry goose.

So yes — golfers are liars. And golf is ridiculous for a thousand reasons.

Still not convinced?

Don't worry. The next few chapters will ensure you finally see the light.

ON THE TEE—WHERE HOPE DIES QUICKLY

1

The first tee is where optimism meets reality. Golfers convince themselves they're prepared. Their playing partners are here to watch the chaos unfold.

There's so much hope on the tee. With a perfect lie and the hole stretched out in front of you, the possibilities feel endless. Birdie? Maybe. Eagle? Sure, why not?

Of course not.

Hope disappears the moment you make an off-balance swipe and send the ball into parts of the course no one's ever seen before. If you're lucky, you'll find it and get to hit it again. If not, you'll have to produce another ball, tee it up, and start the whole ridiculous exercise over.

It'd be bad enough if this only happened once or twice in a round. But no — golf demands that you rinse and repeat this little heartbreak **eighteen** times before finally letting you go home.

And still, we never learn. We stride up to the tee box, full of confidence and optimism. Then we swing, swear, and slink back to the cart.

Over and over again. Round after round.

WHAT'S SAID vs. WHAT'S MEANT

The tee box is prime territory for golf banter. Everyone's close together, so it's easier to talk than while in the fairway (or, more likely, the rough). And, since the hope hasn't been crushed yet, there's still enough confidence in the air for a little trash talk.

Golfers rarely say exactly what they mean. There's a whole unspoken "code" to golf language — and most of it is total nonsense. So, if someone throws one of these lines at you on the tee, here's what they're actually saying.

"Go ahead and let it rip with the driver."
I want to see you launch it so far into the f*****g trees that you'll need a compass just to find your way back.

"Nice wide fairway on this hole."
You couldn't hit the fairway if it was wide enough to land a jet.

"All you need to do is avoid that fairway bunker and you're all set."
That bunker has your name all over it. It's pail and shovel time.

"Not much wind on this hole."
The wind is the least of your problems. You'd miss every fairway in a vacuum.

"With your power, you can reach this par five in two shots."
You'll be lucky to reach the fairway in two shots, let alone the green.

"Swing a little harder. I think you have more in the tank."
I can't wait to watch you fall on your a**e.

"You had the best score on the last hole, so it's your honor."
Watching you hit a horrible tee shot will make me feel better about my chances.

"Don't worry about that pond. You'll carry it easily with your driver."

Kiss that ball before you tee it up — you're never seeing it again.

"Just a slight dogleg to the left on this hole."
Good luck. Every shot you've ever hit goes right... how are you going to make a left turn?

"You can hit a long drive from this elevated tee."
That's just more time in the air for your ball to get even farther from the fairway.

"I just learned this new driver grip you should try."
Because the grip you're using hasn't hit a fairway in weeks.

"Don't worry, those are just first tee jitters."
Said on the 13th hole.

"Go ahead and hit— I don't think you can reach the group in front of us."
What are you waiting for? You couldn't reach them with three drives in a row.

"Imagine this hole is to win the club championship."
There's no way you'll ever qualify for the club championship, let alone win it.

"Slow down and take a deep breath before this one."
A full hour of meditation wouldn't help you hit the short grass.

"I'm impressed you're still using that driver after last round."
You lost four balls, hit three trees, and broke a window.

"Just keep your head down through impact."
So you don't have to see where the ball goes.

"There's no way you can miss the fairway with that perfect stance."
It's your swing that sucks.

"How much money did you spend on that driver?"
How much money did you flush down the toilet?

"If you hit this fairway, lunch is on me."
You're more likely to hit it O.B. — and you're buying lunch.

"How about a friendly wager on who hits the longer drive?"
You might as well just pay me now and save yourself the embarrassment.

"I think you're going to find the fairway this time."
Of course, it won't be the correct fairway.

"Have you ever considered taking lessons for a couple of weeks?"
After the lessons, you should quit the game.

"This course has beautiful trees."
Please stop hitting them — it's a crime against nature.

"I think your driver swing is getting better."
There's no way it could've gotten worse.

"The rough on this course is short, so don't worry about hitting the fairway."
You were never going to hit the fairway — and probably won't even hit the rough, either.

"Do you know anyone else who plays golf around here?"
Go play with them. I'm tired of watching your slice.

"Try taking a practice swing before your tee shot."
Maybe you'll pull a muscle and I won't have to watch you hit the ball.

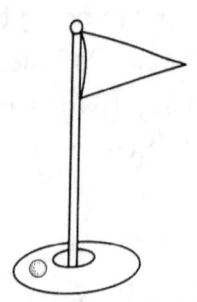

"You'll find it."
That ball's f*****g gone. Never to be seen again. Don't even bother looking!

"With your fade, try aiming down the left side of the fairway."
You don't hit a fade. You hit a slice. And it doesn't matter where you aim — the fairway's safe.

"Do you think that's the right club for this hole?"
It's not. But then again, you don't have the right club.

"Is that a new laser range finder you've got?"
All the gear... no idea.

FAMOUS GOLF FAILS

All of us average golfers are familiar with failing off the tee — over and over again. But what about the pros? They always stripe it right down the middle, right?

Not so much.

Here are a few famous examples of pro golfers losing their way off the tee when it mattered most.

Phil Mickelson — 2006 U.S. Open

There's nothing easy about the U.S. Open, even for a Hall of Famer like Phil Mickelson. He's won basically everything in golf — but never lifted the trophy at his national open.

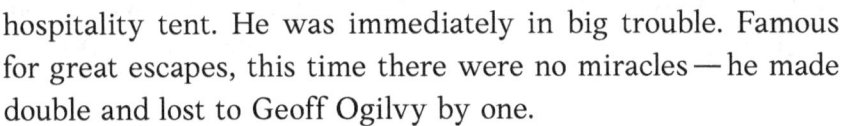

He should have. Standing on the 18th tee at Winged Foot, Phil needed a par for the title. The smart play was a three-wood or long iron. Instead, he chose the driver and hit it directly into the hospitality tent. He was immediately in big trouble. Famous for great escapes, this time there were no miracles — he made double and lost to Geoff Ogilvy by one.

Phil wasn't the only one to blow it. Colin Montgomerie could've won with a par. He made double—and never did win a major. Jim Furyk needed par for a playoff, but made bogey. The 18th at Winged Foot was a bloodbath. Few were spared.

Phil summed it up best in his press conference:
"I just can't believe that I did that. I am such an idiot."

Rory McIlroy—2011 Masters

Every golfer dreams of standing on the 10th tee at The Masters with the lead and only nine holes to play. Rory McIlroy found himself in exactly that spot in 2011. Names like Tiger Woods, Adam Scott, and Jason Day were lurking, but Rory controlled his own destiny on Sunday afternoon.

That dream turned into a nightmare as soon as he hit his tee shot on 10. The hole turns to the left—but Rory turned it way too far left. Deep in the trees with no great options, Rory chopped his way to a triple-bogey seven and fell out of the lead for good. To make matters worse, he four-putted for double on the 12th and was completely out of the running. He went from leading on the 10th tee to finishing the tournament 10 shots off the lead.

None of the big names dotting the leaderboard managed to secure the Green Jacket that day. Instead, Charl Schwartzel took the opportunity Rory left behind and ran with it. He birdied the last four holes of the tournament for a two-shot victory and his only major championship.

Kevin Na — 2011 Texas Open

Famous golf fails usually happen at the biggest tournaments. It's the size of the stage that makes the mistakes stand out. But sometimes, a smaller event delivers a trainwreck so dramatic that it just can't be ignored.

That was the 2011 Texas Open at TPC San Antonio. Kevin Na, a steady PGA Tour player, arrived at the tee of the 9th hole. His tee shot sailed deep into the trees next to the fairway. He had to go back to the tee and hit another one — and it went into the same trees. The downward spiral began from there. Oh, what a spiral it would become.

Deep in the woods, Na took swing after swing, seemingly getting nowhere. Eventually, he made the merciful decision to take a drop for an unplayable lie. But the damage — so much damage — was already done. Unbelievably, he got onto the green in 14, calmly two-putted, and wrote a 16 on his card.

A 16 isn't just rare for a professional. It's rare for anyone. Most players would give up long before reaching that number. Na stuck it out, finished what he started, and claimed a piece of PGA Tour history along the way.

Sergio Garcia — 2013 Players Championship

The 17th hole at TPC Sawgrass — the home of The Players Championship — is no ordinary tee shot. With the green completely surrounded by water, it doesn't matter that the hole is under 150 yards. It still terrifies the best players in the world.

Sergio Garcia stepped up in the 2013 tournament tied with Tiger Woods. Two pars would take him to a playoff. So, he played it safe to the middle of the green, right?

Nope.

He went right at the pin, cut tight to the edge of the water. The shot came up short, splashed, and Sergio was toast.

For good measure, he dumped the next ball in too. He eventually made a quadruple bogey, then doubled 18 for good measure. In about 20 minutes, he went from tied for the lead to six shots behind and a ninth-place finish.

Ouch.

WEIRD GOLF RULES

The rules of golf are complicated. Sure, the goal — shoot the lowest score — is simple. But how you get there? That's where it gets weird. And it starts right on the tee.

- **The height of a tee is limited to four inches.**
  If you want to tee it up knee-high and take a swipe, you're out of luck. Apparently, golf doesn't want baseball players getting too comfortable.

- **If you tee off from the wrong tee box,**
  You have to correct your mistake and take a two-stroke penalty. Honestly, if you can't figure out what hole you're on, that penalty might be deserved.

- **A swing and a miss still counts.**
  If you meant to hit the ball, it's a stroke — even if you came up empty. As if whiffing wasn't painful enough, the rules add insult to injury.

ON THE FAIRWAY (OR MORE LIKELY, THE ROUGH)

2

If you aren't familiar with the term *"fairway"*, allow us to explain. It's that strip of short grass between the deep rough and the towering trees. Some say it's just a myth — and few have actually seen it.

On the rare occasion you do find the fairway, it's easy to feel a little cocky. And why not? You've conquered the tee shot and set yourself up perfectly for a smooth approach and a birdie putt. All that's left to do now... is blow it.

Whether you're sitting pretty in the fairway or knee-deep in rough, your next shot will tell the story of the hole. Even a bad drive can be salvaged by a great second shot. But once that second shot goes horribly wrong? It's over. You'll be writing down a big number and shaking your head all the way to the next tee.

Every golfer dreams of watching their approach shot soar high, land softly on the green, and roll up next to the cup for an easy birdie. It's a beautiful image.

But golf doesn't make dreams come true — it crushes them one crappy swing at a time.

Have fun out there.

WHAT'S SAID vs. WHAT'S MEANT

Golfers never miss a chance to harass each other during a round. It's half the fun. After all, why sign up for four hours of frustration if you can't sling a little trash talk along the way?

Keeping the banter alive in the fairway takes skill, though. With your group spread out all over the place, timing your zingers just right can be tricky.

Here are some you might hear next time you're tracking down your ball in parts unknown.

"Are you thinking about laying up?"
You're going to lay up, whether you try to or not.

"I think your drive might have rolled into the rough."
That's not the rough — that's the wilderness.

"You can stick this approach close to the hole."

It won't be the right hole, but still.

"You might be in the taller grass just past the rough."

Bring your machete — this is going to be an adventure.

"This green is a pretty big target."

Doesn't matter. You haven't hit a green all day — and you're not starting now.

"Do you think this is where your drive ended up?"

Call Search and Rescue. We're never finding this ball alone.

"It might be smart to aim a little left of this pin."

Your irons curve so far right, you'd need to aim backwards to hit the target.

"Look how nice the grass is on this fairway."

Please stop shoveling up chunks of it with your practice swings.

"Make sure to use enough club to get over that bunker."

I've never been more sure of anything than your ball going directly into that bunker.

"You hit such a good drive, I think you can reach this par five in two."
That was your only good drive of the day — and you're about to waste it.

"That's some deep rough."
Your ball is never getting out of there unless you brought a lawn mower.

"I've never seen anyone hit the ball into this position."
You might be the worst golfer I've ever played with.

"Bad luck having your tee shot end up in a divot."
At least now you have an excuse for your sh***y approach.

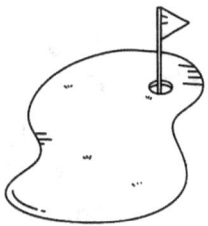

"I think this approach is a little into the wind."
I'm not really trying to help — I just wanted to mess with your head.

"Don't put too much backspin on this wedge shot."
Who am I kidding — you only put sideways spin on the ball.

"Why don't you keep this one low and under the wind?"
By "low," I mean you're going to top it and roll it halfway there.

"It will take a high shot to hold this green."
You don't have a high shot. You don't really have a low shot either.

"This pin is in a dangerous spot. I'd play it safe."
For you, playing it safe means picking up your ball and heading to the clubhouse.

"You took a nice divot on that swing."
I've never seen that much turf fly on one shot.

"Just pitch it out of the trees and get back to the fairway."
We'll be here all day if you keep going for the green.

"You deserved a better lie after that drive."
Your bad luck is making me laugh.

"These fairways are a little soft today."
Now that it's in your head, I can't wait to see you hit this one fat.

"Your ball should be around here somewhere."
It's never coming back. Maybe write it off on your taxes.

"From this position in the fairway, it's birdie time."
Birdie time was hours ago — and you didn't have a reservation.

"Just hit the middle of the green and leave an easy two-putt."
There's no such thing as an easy two-putt for you. Also — you're not hitting the green.

"I think we have a little wind behind us."
That back bunker is calling your name.

"It's hard to play from the rough in these wet conditions."
You should be good at it by now—you've been in there all day.

"Did you check the wind?"
You never check the wind. And it doesn't matter—the ball never gets off the ground.

"Go ahead. I think you're away."
I know you're away—because I've outdriven you on every hole.

"That looks like a tricky lie, but you can handle it."
No, you can't. Stick to playing golf on Xbox.

"How many golf balls do you think are at the bottom of that pond?"
Here comes one more!

"I will never forget that swing you just made."
I wish I could—but it's going to haunt my nightmares.

FAMOUS GOLF FAILS

To be fair, professional golfers hit plenty of great approach shots. It's part of what makes them who they are. You can't shoot scores in the 60s without knocking it close for makeable birdie putts.

That doesn't mean their approaches always go to plan, though. Golf history is littered with failed approach shots — from both the fairway and the rough. Let's dive into a few examples of pros who failed spectacularly on the big stage.

Jean Van de Velde — 1999 Open Championship

Without a doubt, this one tops the list of golf fails. The cream of the crop. The GOAT of meltdowns. It's the fail by which all others are measured.

To be fair, the collapse started on the tee. Needing only a double bogey to win the Open Championship at Carnoustie — not just any course, but one of the toughest in the world — Van de Velde pulled driver and found the rough. Things started to unravel from there. Still, a smart second shot could've settled him down and secured the Claret Jug.

Or not.

Instead of pitching out, Van de Velde went for the green and found a creek. He even considered playing from the water before thinking better of it and taking a drop. A few swipes later, he made triple bogey — and landed in a playoff.

Congratulations, Paul Lawrie. Here's your Open Championship!

Videos of the collapse have racked up hundreds of thousands of views on YouTube — despite the fact that YouTube didn't exist until six years later. Van de Velde played just nine more majors in his career and never finished better than T19.

Surely he hasn't lost any sleep over what could've been... if he'd just pitched out and made double to win.

Sergio Garcia — 2018 Masters

The 2017 Masters was the crowning achievement of Sergio Garcia's career. Long considered the "Best Player Never to Win a Major," he finally shed the label and claimed the Green Jacket.

But golf doesn't let anyone stay on top for long.

In his very first round as defending champion, Garcia reached the par-5 15th needing something good to happen. It didn't. His drive was solid — but the hole fell apart in spectacular fashion.

Going for the green in two, he came up short and found the water. Not ideal, but not unheard of.

Then came the real disaster.

Drop. Water. Drop. Water. Drop. Water. Drop. Water. Drop. Finally... dry land.

After dunking nearly a half-dozen balls in the pond, Sergio strolled up to the green and rolled in a ten-footer — for a **13**. It was the highest score ever recorded on that hole, and one of the worst in major championship history.

At least after missing the cut, his Green Jacket was still waiting for him in the locker when he packed up and went home.

Dustin Johnson — 2023 U.S. Open

Heading into the 2023 U.S. Open, Dustin Johnson was a favorite. He'd played plenty of golf in Southern California, and the event was being held at Los Angeles Country Club. A first-round 64 only raised expectations — he looked primed to win his second U.S. Open title.

Then the golf gods intervened.

It started quietly. On the second hole of round two, DJ found a fairway bunker. Not ideal, but manageable for a player of his caliber. All he needed was a simple lay-up and a chance to save par.

Sounds easy. It wasn't.

His bunker shot veered left into the long rough. His next shot barely got airborne and failed to clear the hazard. After a drop, he flew the green, chipped back on, and two-putted for a **quadruple bogey eight**.

To his credit, DJ fought back and finished the day at even par. He ended the week T10, seven shots behind the winner. But things could've looked very different if not for one disastrous hole that seemed to come out of nowhere.

WEIRD GOLF RULES

Many of golf's strangest rules show up in the fairways, rough, trees — and beyond. It's a big world out there, and the rulebook has to cover every situation imaginable. Even if you know the rules pretty well, one or two of these might still surprise you:

- **You can't move your ball out of a divot.**
  If some hacker in the group ahead laid the sod over one and left a canyon in the fairway — tough luck. Play it as it lies!

○ **You can move your ball out of an animal hole.**
If a burrowing critter made the hole, you're allowed relief. If it was a human animal with a sand wedge? No such luck.

○ **Hitting the wrong ball is a two-stroke penalty.**
If you hack one out of the rough only to realize it's not yours, enjoy those extra strokes — and you still have to find your actual ball.

○ **You get relief for an embedded ball... sometimes.**
If it's plugged in its own pitch mark in the fairway, you're entitled to relief. But the same lie in the rough? Play it as it lies. At this point, it feels like the rules are just messing with you.

SHORT GAME— CHUNKS, BLADES, & TOTAL MELTDOWNS

3

You'd think golf would get easier as you get closer to the hole.

You'd be wrong.

Somehow, short shots are even harder than long shots — and those are already hard enough. The punishment golf can dish out truly knows no limits.

The embarrassment possible around the green is unmatched. It's understandable to miss a fairway with a driver. But to flub a chip when you're just a few feet from the green? That's brutal. You look like an idiot — there's really no other way to say it.

Emotional outbursts are also common in this part of the game. Who among us hasn't chucked a wedge back toward the cart — or into a pond — after a particularly lousy pitch? These shots look so easy, but they're deceptively difficult. And when it all goes wrong, it's tough not to lose your mind. Will you improve your short game anytime soon?

Probably not.

You're destined to suffer around the greens like the rest of us — so we might as well laugh about it along the way.

WHAT'S SAID vs. WHAT'S MEANT

After a long journey from the tee to somewhere near the green, the group finally comes back together — united in a desperate attempt to finish the hole strong.

The banter picks up again here, and it's often particularly ruthless. Short game shots are hard enough when you're alone. They're almost impossible when someone's talking trash in your ear.

Heard any of these comments before you hit a chip or pitch lately?

Don't take them at face value — here's what they really mean.

"This looks like a perfect spot for a chip and run."
With your short game, it'll be more like
a chunk and pray.

"You need a nice, delicate touch to stop this chip close to the hole."
You have all the finesse of a bowling ball rolling down a flight of stairs.

"Don't take too much grass on this one."
Your chip shots look like you're competing in a deepest divot contest.

"It's okay—everyone hits a bad chip from time to time."
You're not good enough to be getting that mad.

"I think you moved your head a little early on that one."
Of course, you move your head early on every chip.

"You got a great lie for this chip."
I can't wait to see how you're going to blow it.

"Watch out for the slope behind the hole."
This one's going to roll off the other side, and you'll be chipping again.

"Knock it up there for a gimme."
I'm not giving it to you—no matter how close you chip it.

"That's a chip shot you could make."
Well... not you. But a good golfer could.

42

"Make sure not to hit this one fat."

You're going to hit it so thin it'll never leave the ground.

"I think chipping is the most important part of the whole game."

Just trying to make you feel worse about how bad you are at it.

"Want to have a chipping contest?"

I know I'm not great — but I'm still way better than you.

"Do you think that's the right club for this chip?"

Now that you're overthinking it, a chunk is guaranteed.

"The ball is sitting down a bit in the rough for this one."

Hope you brought a fu**ing shovel.

"Do you get nervous before tricky chip shots?"

You do now.

"Take a deep breath and relax before hitting this chip."
I can see your hands shaking. Need a second?

"I bet you'll get some nice spin on this chip shot."
You won't. But now you're thinking about it, and that's fun for me.

"I think you can get this one close."
As long as 30 feet counts as close.

"Great players have great short games."
And you, of course, are not a great player.

"I've never seen anyone get up and down from that spot."
And you're not nearly as good as the people who have.

"Don't worry, I'm sure you'll get this one up and down."
That takes a good chip and a good putt. You can't do either.

"It's not very often you have to chip over a bunker."
Not that it matters — you're chipping into it anyway.

"I don't think I've ever seen you blade a chip shot."
There's a first time for everything.

"Have you ever seen anyone chip the ball into the water?"
I've got a front row seat and I can't wait.

"How often do you work on your short game?"
Never mind. I can tell the answer is never.

"The lob wedge can get out of any situation."
When someone else is swinging it.

"It's always good to leave an uphill putt after a chip shot."
In your case, just be happy if you're putting at all.

"Have you ever heard of 'thin to win'?"

In your case, it might be more like 'top it and drop it.'

"Your ball is sitting up nicely on top of the grass."

Which means you're about to go right under it and whiff.

"You'll need some soft hands for this one."

My cracked iPhone screen has better touch than you.

"Hitting a chip shot fat is just the worst feeling."

And I don't even feel bad about putting that thought in your head.

FAMOUS GOLF FAILS

Watching professional golf can be annoying. The players stroll around the course making it look easy—while wearing pants that cost more than your entire set of clubs. Even when they miss a green, they usually just chip it close and tap it in. It's insufferable.

So there's no shame in taking great pleasure when a terrible short-game shot derails a pro's hopes of winning. Why can't they suffer like the rest of us once in a while?

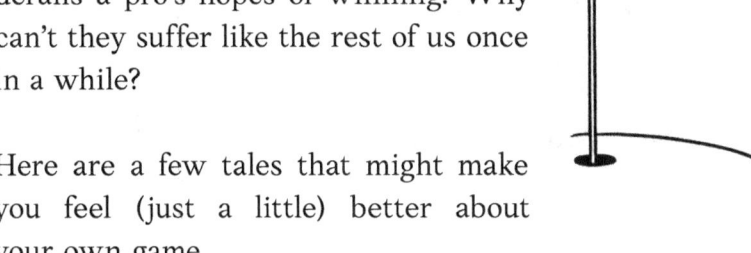

Here are a few tales that might make you feel (just a little) better about your own game.

Hunter Mahan—2010 Ryder Cup

There's no pressure in golf quite like the Ryder Cup. With the weight of a country—or a continent—on a player's shoulders, even routine shots can become monumental challenges. Just ask Hunter Mahan.

In 2010, Mahan was matched up with Graeme McDowell for the Sunday singles match. The overall score was tied, and everything came down to these two players. By the time they reached the 17th, Mahan was two down with two to play. He needed to win both holes to tie.

He didn't.

Facing a relatively basic chip shot—one he was likely trying to hole—Mahan suddenly turned into a 15-handicapper. From a perfect lie, he completely flubbed it and didn't even get the ball onto the green.

The match—and the Ryder Cup—was over just like that. On the biggest stage, in front of the largest audience in golf, his short game vanished.

Golf is a cruel mistress.

Viktor Hovland—2022 Masters

Viktor Hovland has always been honest about his chipping: it sucks. He's never hidden the fact that it's the weakest part of his game. Yet somehow, despite this glaring flaw, he's become one of the best players in the world.

But chipping at Augusta National is no joke. The lightning-fast greens leave no margin for error.

That reality hit hard in round two of the 2022 Masters. On the very first hole of the day, Hovland faced a fairly routine pitch. Most pros would get up and down from there. Hovland had other ideas.

The ball shot up the face of his wedge and barely traveled half the distance to the target. Now, from a similar spot, he had to try again. That chip wasn't great either. He walked away with a double bogey.

The rough start led to a 76 and knocked him out of contention for the week. And somewhere on that walk to the second tee, Hovland was likely thinking what so many hackers have muttered before:

"If only I could chip..."

Scottie Scheffler — 2022 J.P. McManus Pro-Am

When a professional golfer botches a chip shot, it's easy to blame nerves. After all, pros play under tremendous pressure — and chip shots (and putts) are where that pressure really shows up.

That's why it's so refreshing to see a pro blow it when nerves aren't even a factor.

Scottie Scheffler — one of the very best in the world — was playing in the J.P. McManus Pro-Am, which is hardly a pressure cooker like a major or the Ryder Cup. As he prepared for a flop shot from the side of the green, a crowd gathered close to watch one of the top players in the world do his thing.

They didn't realize they might want to take a step or two back.

Instead of lofting the ball gently onto the green, Scheffler hit a cold shank — and just about nailed the cameraman right between the eyes. No one was harmed, and given the low-stakes setting, everyone (including Scheffler) had a good laugh.

Justin Thomas — 2023 Open Championship

The Open Championship presents unique short-game challenges. No lush grass. No fluffy lies. Players have to get creative with low, skidding chips — and not everyone makes the adjustment.

Justin Thomas, for example.

In round one of the 2023 Open, on the very first hole, Thomas missed the green and ended up just short of a pot bunker. He needed to chip over it and onto the green.

That was the plan.

Instead, he pitched the ball directly into the face of the bunker, and it rolled right back into the sand. To be fair, he was probably just an inch or two from pulling it off. But in golf, an inch might as well be a mile.

He shot a shocking 82. Even a solid 71 on Friday wasn't enough to get him to the weekend. Sometimes, it all goes wrong on the very first hole.

WEIRD GOLF RULES

Every once in a while, the rules of golf can actually help you. If you know how to use them, they might even provide a break from the suffering.

But not usually.

Most of the time, the rules just make your problems worse. Were you familiar with these unusual ones that apply to shots around the green?

- **Hitting the ball twice in a single swing when chipping only counts as one stroke.** A rare moment when the rules aren't out to get us. Maybe this game doesn't hate us after all!

○ **If you cause the ball to move when taking your stance in the rough, you have to replace it and take a one-stroke penalty.**
Okay — golf does hate us, just as we thought.

○ **If your chip or pitch lands on a sprinkler head or drain and bounces somewhere ridiculous, tough luck.**
You don't get a replay. You have to play it as it lies.

How is that fair?!

BUNKER BANTER—
EXCUSES FROM THE SAND

4

Golf is played on grass.

Except when it isn't.

For some reason — and who knows why — golf courses are also littered with little pits of sand scattered across the landscape. They're called bunkers. Probably because once you're in one, you'd rather hunker down and hide than try to hit your ball again.

There are greenside bunkers. There are fairway bunkers. They all suck.

Not only do you have to hit a shot from a soft, squishy surface, but you also get the added joy of raking up after yourself when you're done. What is this — your part-time job? As if smoothing out the sand is going to help anyone. Raked or not, we're all screwed in the bunker.

Adding to the misery is the fact that it might take multiple swings just to get out. Even the worst golfer usually makes some kind of progress from the grass. But from the sand? Not guaranteed. You might swing again and again... and again... only to watch the ball roll right back to your feet.

What a game!

WHAT'S SAID vs. WHAT'S MEANT

When you're stuck in the sand, you're an easy target. Your playing partners know you're in trouble — and they can't wait to pile on.

Their comments might sound like encouragement, but don't be fooled. They're loving every second of your sandy misery.

Below are some of the "helpful" things you might hear as you climb down into the bunker for yet another doomed attempt to get out in one swing. Once you've read through this list, you'll know exactly what they *really* mean.

"Bunker shots are so unpredictable."
Who knows where this one's going?

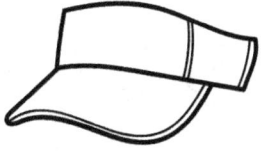

"Remember to take a big swing to get the ball out of the sand."
You're not getting out — and I want to see you dig a trench.

"That's the easiest bunker shot you can have."
Easy or not, you'll be throwing the ball out after a few failed swipes.

57

"You got a perfect lie in the bunker."
There are no excuses for a bad shot — but you'll still think of some.

"I think bunker shots are the best part of your game."
In other words, you suck at everything.

"Ouch — it looks like your ball is buried in the bunker."
Hahahahahahahaha.

"Did you practice any bunker shots before we teed off?"
Even if you did, it clearly didn't help.

"You'll need a high shot to get it over the lip of that bunker."
Watch out — this one's coming right back at you.

"Keep your head down on this one."
So you can get even more sand in your eyes.

"That sand looks a little wet—make sure to get under it."
Everyone on the other side of the green better duck. This one's coming in hot.

"Want me to rake that bunker for you?"
With how many swings you've taken, it's the least I can do.

"Make sure to avoid that front bunker—it's a deep one."
Now that I've mentioned it, there's only one place this ball is going.

"You took a lot of sand out of the trap with that swing."
Check the bottom of your divot—I think you struck oil.

"The lob wedge can get out of any situation."
When someone else is swinging it.

"How many swings have you made down in that trap?"
If you blast out any more sand, you'll never crawl back out.

59

"Do you want me to grab your other wedge?"
Doesn't matter how many wedges you try — nothing's helping you now.

"Make sure to wiggle your feet in for a good stance."
You'll be picking sand out of your toes for weeks.

"Your bunker shots are usually better than that one."
And your usual ones are awful.

"That sand looks really soft and smooth."
Here's a beach towel — you'll be in there a while.

"A thin bunker shot can really fly."
Heads up — there are people on the next tee.

"That shot buried itself deep in the bunker."
Let's just call your ball 'The Undertaker' from now on.

"Only a perfect swing will get you out of this bunker."
Remind me — when was the last time you hit a perfect shot?

"The best way to escape a bunker is to splash the sand out from under the ball."
Speaking of splash — there's a pond right behind the green.

"You've spent a lot of time in the sand today."
Might want to update your relationship status with bunkers to 'It's Complicated.'

"It might be tough to get out of that trap."
Want a pail and shovel? You can build a castle.

"Practice makes perfect on bunker shots."
In your case, practice might just make you worse.

"Close out this round with a nice bunker save."
If you hit this thin, the clubhouse windows are toast.

"Did you know it's possible to putt out of a bunker if it has a low lip?"
Please try it. I can't take any more of your wedge work.

"You've dug a lot of sand out of that trap."
Your new nickname is 'The Archaeologist.'

"The bunkers are deep on this course."
Almost as deep as the debt you're in from trying to buy a better golf game.

"Go ahead and hit your bunker shot while I look for my ball."
If you want to throw it out and pretend, I won't say a word.

"With that lie in the sand, you'll really need to hit down on this shot."
Let me know if you find any fossils while you're in there.

FAMOUS GOLF FAILS

The gap between professional golfers and the rest of us is huge in every part of the game. They hit it farther, putt it better, and they get paid very handsomely to do it.

That said, the gap might be biggest in the sand.

Get this: pros will sometimes hit the ball into the bunker *on purpose*. That's pure insanity to a normal golfer, but to the best in the world, a greenside bunker shot is easy money.

Want to feel just a little better about that? Let's look at a few times when the sand turned a professional into a schmuck — just like the rest of us.

Dustin Johnson — 2010 PGA Championship

It's every golfer's dream: standing on the 18th tee of a major, needing just a par to win. That was Dustin Johnson's reality at the 2010 PGA Championship.

But his tee shot was not a dream. It sailed way right, into a sandy area miles from the fairway — and even farther from the green. Johnson found the ball, laid up short of the green, and figured he needed to get up and down for the title.

Or so he thought.

Turns out he had unknowingly grounded his club in a bunker. While it looked like a waste area, the rules for the week defined it as a proper bunker. That meant grounding the club was a two-stroke penalty.

Instead of joining Martin Kaymer and Bubba Watson in a playoff, Johnson was suddenly tied for fifth — and headed home after one of the most confusing and painful rules infractions in golf history.

Jeff Maggert — 2003 Masters

Jeff Maggert's PGA Tour career might not have been record-breaking, but it was definitely successful. He played for years, stayed competitive, and racked up millions in earnings along the way. Not a bad gig.

His best shot at winning a major probably came at the 2003 Masters. Leading by a single shot on Sunday, Maggert stood on the third tee of a short par four with everything in front of him. He found a fairway bunker off the tee — not ideal, but manageable.

Then it all went wrong.

His approach drilled the face of the bunker and came flying right back at him. Despite his best efforts, the ball struck him before settling back into the sand. At the time, that was a two-stroke penalty.

He walked off with a triple bogey and never held the lead again. He finished in fifth place.

Sadly, they don't give out green jackets for fifth.

Jack Nicklaus — 1995 Open Championship

Only two names really come up when debating the greatest golfer of all time: Jack Nicklaus and Tiger Woods. We won't settle that here — but we can highlight a time when even Jack reminded us that golf is a savage game.

It was the 1995 Open Championship at St. Andrews — the Home of Golf. Nicklaus was past his prime, but still fully capable of brilliance when things clicked. Then came the 14th hole in the first round.

The hole? A par five.

The danger? A monster called Hell Bunker.

Nicklaus found it with his second shot. It took him four tries to escape. Once on the green, he promptly three-putted for a **ten**.

Even the Golden Bear wasn't immune to the nightmare that is a deep bunker. It wasn't a common sight during his legendary career — but for once, Jack felt the pain we all know too well.

Sepp Straka — 2024 U.S. Open

Every golfer knows the game isn't fair. Sometimes it only takes a single round — or just a few holes — for something to happen that leaves you shaking your head in disbelief.

For Sepp Straka at the 2024 U.S. Open, it probably felt even less fair than usual.

After a solid drive on the 382-yard par-4 third hole, Straka had a straightforward approach. No shot at the U.S. Open is truly "easy," but this one wasn't too bad. His 139-yard wedge was right on target — maybe a little *too* on target.

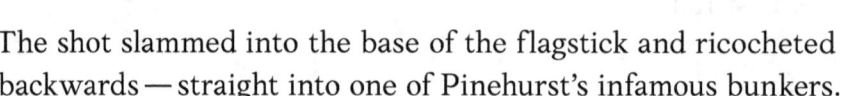

The shot slammed into the base of the flagstick and ricocheted backwards — straight into one of Pinehurst's infamous bunkers.

Ouch.

What looked like a birdie chance instantly turned into a scramble.

Then came the bunker shot: it came out hot, skipped across the green, and stopped in the long grass on the other side. He had a chance to salvage the hole from there — but that went wrong too. Once that happened, it was game over.

When all was said and done, a **seven** went on the card, and Straka tumbled down the leaderboard.

He did well to hang on and make the cut, but finished T56 — and never had a shot at contending after that bunker-related mess.

WEIRD GOLF RULES

If there's anywhere on the course you could use a break from the rules, it's in the bunker. Can't you get a little help when you're deep in the trap with no way out? Nope. These bizarre rules below just show how the game is really out to get all of us.

- **You can't touch the sand with your club to check its condition before hitting a shot, or you will incur a two stroke penalty.**
  Is the sand as soft as a pillow or as hard as a rock? Who knows! Every bunker shot is a fun (and terrifying) surprise.

○ **There is no relief from a footprint in the sand before hitting your shot.**
Some moron in the group in front of you didn't bother to rake the bunker? Tough luck, sucker!

○ **The rules allow for relief from a plugged lie in the fairway. In the bunker? Not so much.**
Play it as it lies. Spoiler alert — your next shot will probably be played from the sand as well.

THE GREEN — THE LAND OF BROKEN DREAMS

5

Nowhere else in sports does the perception of a task break so dramatically from reality. On the greens of a golf course, the job seems simple—rudimentary, even. Roll a ball across perfectly manicured grass and watch it drop into a hole.

How hard could it be?

When you watch a pro smash a 300-yard drive, it's obvious how much athleticism it takes—and you can probably accept why you can't do the same. In other sports, you can watch a sprinter blaze through the 100 meters or a basketball player throw down a monster dunk and know those feats are simply out of reach.

But making a 10-footer for birdie? Why *can't* that be you?

All it takes is standing still and moving a small stick back and forth a few inches. It's the kind of motion you could teach a toddler.

Yet we still suck.

Watching amateurs on the practice green is almost as painful as watching them on the range. Every round feels like it'll be the one where our magical putting touch finally shows up.

Every round ends the same: disappointment.

Rinse. Repeat.

We've all seen the movie — and somehow, we keep buying a ticket.

And we haven't even mentioned the yips yet. Yes, the yips. They are real, and they are a disaster. A golfer with the yips can turn a six-inch putt into a psychological thriller.

Even worse? Most of them *don't quit*.

They just keep showing up, putter in hand, ready to suffer all over again. Just give up already. Walk away. Reclaim your life.

WHAT'S SAID vs. WHAT'S MEANT

Banter on the greens is one of the best parts of golf. With the hole wrapping up — and maybe a wager or two hanging in the balance — the pressure is at its peak. Sometimes, all it takes is one well-timed jab to get in your opponent's head and turn a make into a miss.

The most skilled trash-talkers know how to play it subtle. What they say won't sound too bad — it might even seem encouraging. But it's not.

Below is a collection of the "friendly" things you'll hear on the greens from your so-called golf buddies — and what they really mean.

"Maybe take some speed off of this next putt."
Your putter has more clubhead speed than your driver today.

"Long putts are always tough."
When I said this was a par five, I didn't mean five putts.

"Don't worry — take the time you need to get a good read."
Hurry the f**k up.

"That one came up just a bit short."
Is your putter on power-saving mode?

"I'm surprised that didn't break more."
You got closer to the bunker than the hole.

"You missed the line on that one."
You read putts like my grandma reads texts — slow and completely wrong.

"No pressure— just knock it in."

There's obviously pressure. And you're clearly feeling it.

"Putting in the wind is never easy."

I think that last gust just blew away what was left of your confidence.

"Just needed one more roll out of that one."

Seriously, how many times are you going to leave it short? Do you not want to wake up the grass?

"You are away, so go ahead and go first."

Like, now. Stop reading the putt. Are we filming a documentary here?

"Your outfit looks sharp today."

Notice how I didn't say anything about your putting. Because, oof.

"If only the hole was just a little bit bigger."
That putt still would've missed by a mile.

"Did you buy a lottery ticket before our tee time this morning?"
You'd have a better shot at that than making this putt.

"Treat your putts like they don't matter and you'll make more."
Yours really don't matter — because you're putting for a nine.

"Nothing's more frustrating than three-putting."
Except watching you three-putt all day.

"Do you want to try my putter?"
Yours clearly isn't working. At all.

"When was the last time you made a long putt for birdie?"
We play every week.
I honestly can't remember.
Was it this century?

"You've made every putt all day long."
F**k you.

"That one needs to settle down."
Were you trying to start your next hole early?

"These greens are perfectly smooth."
So what's your excuse?

"Go ahead and tap that one in so we can keep moving."
This hole has lasted longer than your first marriage.

"I can't believe that putt came up short."
Take the headcover off the putter next time.

"That putt looked great — I can't believe it lipped out."
Hahahahahahahaha.

"The greens are giving you some trouble today."
Maybe switch to bowling — at least there are 10 targets to hit.

"Three-footers can be tricky."
My toddler would've knocked that one in.

"You should've practiced some long putts during warm-up."
Wouldn't have mattered. You've got all the touch of a rhinoceros.

"Just keep your head still and you'll be fine."
You look up so fast, I thought there was a naked lady on the next tee.

"Was that a three-putt or a four-putt?"
I'll grab my phone so you can use the calculator.

"That's close enough, I'll give you that one."
Please don't make me watch any more of this s**t.

"Try to be aggressive with this uphill putt."
I can't wait to see you blast the downhill comebacker past the hole.

"The grain is pretty strong on these greens."
You don't even know what grain is, let alone how to read it.

"Try relaxing your grip a little bit."
I can see the veins in your hands about to explode.

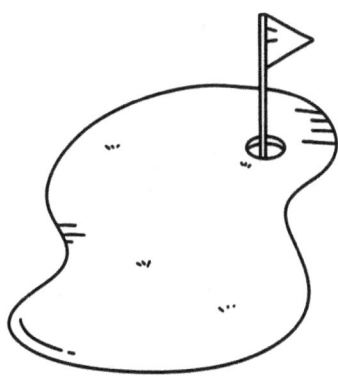

FAMOUS GOLF FAILS

Even professional golfers aren't immune to disasters on the green. Some of the most painful fails in the history of the game have happened with a putter in hand, and the whole world watching.

These stories prove one thing for sure: when it comes to the flatstick, golf plays no favorites.

Scott Hoch — 1989 Masters

If there's one scenario that every golfer has played out in their imagination, it's this: two feet to win the Masters. That's exactly where Scott Hoch found himself in 1989, in a playoff with Nick Faldo. One short putt for a Green Jacket.

Faldo was standing off to the side, probably already accepting defeat.

Hoch took his time. He stalked the putt from every angle — far more than you'd expect for a two-footer. But who could blame him? This was the biggest moment of his career. All he had to do was knock it in and claim golf immortality.

Then he missed. Badly.

He jabbed at it, missed left, and ran it at least three feet past the hole. The golf world was stunned. To his credit, Hoch composed himself and sank the next putt to stay alive.

But that was all Faldo needed. He drained a long birdie putt on the next playoff hole and claimed the title.

Hoch never got that close to winning a major again. And that miss? It's now burned into golf history.

Doug Sanders — 1970 Open Championship

Scott Hoch isn't alone in the club of heartbreaking missed short putts. Doug Sanders joined decades earlier, at none other than St. Andrews.

On the 18th green, Sanders needed to make a putt of less than three feet to win the Open Championship and claim the Claret Jug.

He missed. And not by a little.

Like Hoch, his putt wasn't even close — this time missing to the right. For a moment, it looked like Sanders was about to reach out with his putter and pull the ball back like some frustrated weekend hacker. Now *that* would've made history.

Instead of lifting the trophy, Sanders found himself in an 18-hole playoff the next day against Jack Nicklaus. He held his own, but not quite well enough. Nicklaus won by a single stroke.

Just like Hoch, Sanders never won a major. And just like Hoch, one short putt came to define his career.

Stewart Cink — 2001 U.S. Open

Few finishing holes in major championship history have seen as many twists as the 72nd hole at the 2001 U.S. Open.

Stewart Cink was tied with Retief Goosen playing the final hole. Cink's approach shot sailed long, and after a chip to 15 feet, he missed the par putt and left himself two feet short. The tournament seemed out of reach.

Cink stepped up to tap in — just to clear the stage for Goosen. But somehow, he missed. He tapped in for bogey and walked off dejected, ready to watch Goosen claim the title.

That's not what happened.

Goosen hit his first putt too hard, then missed the comebacker. Just like that, the win slipped away, and he was headed to a playoff with Mark Brooks.

Cink, however, missed that playoff entirely — thanks to a short, rushed putt that he thought didn't matter anymore.

Brandt Snedeker — 2009 BMW Championship

Not all professional golfers are great putters. Like athletes in any sport, golfers have strengths and weaknesses. Some are elite off the tee, others are wizards with an iron, and some dominate around the greens.

Brandt Snedeker was a great putter. It was the cornerstone of his game — the thing that kept him competitive on the PGA Tour.

So when he reached the final hole of the 2009 BMW Championship needing just a two-putt from 15 feet to secure a spot in the Tour Championship, it felt like a done deal. For someone with Snedeker's putting skills, that was as close to a sure thing as you'll find in golf.

The good news? He didn't three-putt.

The bad news? He didn't two-putt either.

One putt? Nope.

Incredibly, he **four-putted** — and just like that his most trusted club betrayed him at the worst possible time, costing him a place in the season finale.

WEIRD GOLF RULES

With just a few feet left to the cup, you might think nothing could go wrong. But why would golf start making sense now? It's been ruthless the whole way, and the rules don't let up just because the grass gets shorter.

Here are a few green-side rules that are just waiting to ruin your day:

- **Don't rub the green.**
  Seriously. It's against the rules to rub your hand on the green to "feel" the texture or speed. That's a two-stroke penalty. But go ahead and fix a ball mark or a spike mark — that's perfectly fine. Who comes up with this stuff?

- **If the ball bounces out of the cup, it doesn't count.**
  You finally drain a perfect putt... and then it pops back out? Sorry — do it again. Because *of course* that doesn't count.

- **Wind can blow your ball to a worse spot.**
  Even if you've marked, cleaned, and replaced your ball — if the wind sends it rolling down a slope? Too bad. You don't get to move it back. Play it from wherever it ended up, sucker.

- **Your ball has 10 seconds to fall in.**
  Yes, this is real. If your ball teeters on the edge of the cup, you only get 10 seconds after walking up to it for it to drop and still count. If it falls in after that? Add a stroke. Absolute evil.

THE 18TH HOLE — WHEN THE WHEELS COME OFF 6

The 18th tee is a place of mixed emotions. On one hand, you've been looking forward to this round all week — and now it's almost over. On the other hand, golf is a merciless game, and you've just spent the last few hours rummaging through the woods for the final few balls in your bag. Your legs are toast, you're regretting not paying for a cart, and a hot meal with a cold drink is sounding better by the second. When does this nightmare end?

Of course, the round isn't actually over when you reach the 18th tee. You've still got one more hole to survive — and there's plenty of time for everything to go horribly wrong. The finish line is both tantalizingly close and impossibly far away.

It's probably that extra bit of pressure that makes the 18th such prime real estate for total disasters. And it's not just amateurs — pros blow it here, too. Whether it's a shot at a major championship or a desperate attempt to finally break 100, the tension is real. That's what makes the 18th so entertaining... and why half the clubhouse lingers on the patio afterward to watch the carnage unfold.

WHAT'S SAID vs. WHAT'S MEANT

The 18th is your final shot at dishing out some trash talk — and players know it. That means the banter here is often the sharpest, most aggressive, and usually the funniest of the day. It also helps that everyone's had four or five hours (and maybe a few drinks) to get fully "loosened up."

So, when someone in your group sidles up with a "friendly" comment on the last hole, here's what they probably *really* mean:

"You've had a tough round, I'd love to see you finish with a par."
I'm so tired of watching you suck. Please, just hit one decent shot.

"I'm sure those people behind the green aren't watching."
They are definitely watching, and they want you to fail.

"Thanks for playing with me today."
We are never doing this again.

89

"This is a tough finishing hole."
Just think about how badly you've played the easy ones. What's going to happen now?

"Watch out for the water to the right."
You probably should, because that's exactly where your ball is going.

"We've had a good match today."
And I'm only saying that because I'm about to win.

"Are you getting tired?"
It sure looks like it. Although your swing on the first hole was pretty sh**y too.*

"The pressure of the last hole is what makes golf exciting."
It's exciting for me to watch you choke.

"Should we grab some lunch after the round?"
You're buying. And I'm starving.

"I hope you saved your best for last."

That must be the plan, because nothing else has looked good.

"Why do they always make the last hole so hard?"

I'm sure you'll butcher it, just like the previous 17.

"Have you ever birdied the last hole?"

You're definitely not starting today.

"I love how the approach shot is downhill to the 18th green."

Use less club. You're about to drop this one in that lady's soup.

"Our match is tied with just the 18th to play."

You can't even golf under normal conditions, let alone pressure.

"It feels so good to finish on a birdie."

Not that you'd know.

"Everything is on the line on this hole."

Ready to fail one last time?

"As soon as we finish, we should book tee times for next week."

At different courses. With different people.

"If you make this putt, you'll remember it all week."

But miss it, and you'll relive the trauma all year.

"It's weird for a course to end with a par three."

Though for you, every hole plays like a par five.

"Don't you think you should hit your driver one more time?"

I want to watch you lose one last ball for the road.

"You just need one more par to break 90."

Honestly, I'll be shocked if you break 100.

"Are you nervous with the parking lot so close to the fairway?"
You should be. I'll go call the windshield repair guy now.

"This has been fun. We should do it again."
Watching you struggle makes me feel better about my game.

"It was quite a challenge playing the back tees today."
You had no business back there. Or out here.

"Just get it up and down and you'll break 100."
With that on your mind, this will be your worst chip of the day.

"I haven't seen you hit a shot that bad all day."
What the f**k was that?

"Take a deep breath and make one more good swing."
You're shaking like you owe the mob money. Speaking of which, you owe me money.

> **"I think this hole plays to your strengths."**

Wait, no. I meant weaknesses. You don't have strengths.

> **"Do you think this round will make your handicap go up?"**

Can it even go any higher?

> **"Nice drive. Now hit the green and make one last putt."**

More likely, hit the clubhouse, take a drop, and three-putt in shame.

FAMOUS GOLF FAILS

When it goes right, the 18th hole — especially in the final round of a tournament — can turn a professional golfer into a hero. A birdie to win on the last hole? That's the stuff legends are made of. But when it goes wrong? Those memories stick around for *ten* lifetimes. Here are a few infamous 18th-hole disasters that these pros are still probably losing sleep over.

Robert Garrigus — 2010 St. Jude Classic

Getting into position to win on the PGA Tour is no small feat. At the 2010 St. Jude Classic, Robert Garrigus had done the hard part — he arrived at the 72nd hole with a three-shot lead. Even a double bogey would've been enough to take home the trophy. Oh, and more than a million dollars. No big deal.

Well... of course it's a big deal. And when something *is* a big deal, even the best players can look awfully silly.

Garrigus chunked his tee shot into the water. After a drop, he pulled his next shot left into the trees. A chip out, approach shot, and two putts later — triple bogey. That dropped him into a playoff with Lee Westwood.

He made bogey on the first playoff hole and handed Westwood the win, completing one of the most memorable final-hole collapses in PGA Tour history.

Adam Scott — 2012 Open Championship

For most of his career, Adam Scott has resembled the closest thing golf has to a robot. His swing? Flawless. His demeanor? Unshakable. His looks? Annoyingly handsome. Seriously — why does one guy get all the luck?

Anyone who felt a tinge of jealousy toward Adam Scott likely enjoyed the way his 2012 Open Championship played out. For most of the week, it was perfection. With only four holes left, Scott had a four-shot lead. Surely, such a golf machine couldn't blow it from there.

Anyone with a hint of jealousy toward Scott probably enjoyed how the 2012 Open Championship played out. For most of the week, he was untouchable. With just four holes to play, he held a four-shot lead. Surely, a machine like that couldn't blow it... right?

Golf had other ideas.

Bogey on 15. Bogey on 16. Bogey on 17. Suddenly, that lead was down to one. Still, just a par on 18 would seal the deal.

Nope. One last bogey dropped him into a tie with Ernie Els, and he would lose the playoff. Sixty-eight holes of brilliant golf undone by four brutal ones — and now his name lives on in the Hall of Heartbreak.

Ed Sneed — 1979 Masters

If you aren't familiar with the name Ed Sneed, don't worry — most golf fans today don't remember this pro from the '70s. He never won a major, and only posted two career top-10 finishes in them. One of those was the 1979 Masters, and while he finished T2, it felt more like heartbreak than achievement. Sneed should have taken home the title — and a place in golf history.

Starting the final round, he held a five-shot lead. That kind of cushion is rare in a major, unless your name is Woods or Nicklaus. He held the lead most of the day and walked to the 16th tee still up by three.

Then came the bogeys.

One on 16. One on 17. Now, like Adam Scott at the Open Championship decades later, Sneed needed to par the 18th to win.

He didn't.

One more bogey dropped him into a playoff with Tom Watson and Fuzzy Zoeller. Zoeller won it. Sneed faded into a footnote, instead of becoming the headline. Golf can be a cruel, cruel game.

WEIRD GOLF RULES

The rules of golf apply equally to all 18 holes, so you don't need to know anything specific when playing the final hole of the day. Of course, that means the rules are just as cruel and illogical here as they are everywhere else. Since many courses have an 18th hole that features a water hazard, let's take a look at some odd rules specifically related to ponds, creeks, rivers, and lakes.

- **You need to see a splash.**
  Even if you *think* your ball went into the water, you can't just assume it. Someone in your group has to *see* it happen. If not, it's considered a lost ball, and you're marching back to replay your shot from the original spot. Yes — really. Hope you were paying attention.

- **No relief allowed from water hazard stakes.**
  Did you get a lucky break and have your ball stop near the edge of the water without going in? The joy might be temporary, because if one of the hazard stakes is in your way, no relief is allowed and you have to play it as it lies. (And pray you don't join your ball in the drink.)

- **You can play it from the water.**
  If your ball is in the water but still playable, feel free to hit it out! You'll completely ruin your pants, and the rest of your day, but at least you (might) save yourself a stroke. On the other hand, you might fail to get the ball out of the water, take a swim, and look like a complete idiot. It's up to you.

THE CLUBHOUSE— WHERE EVERYONE IS A HERO 7

At many golf courses, the clubhouse is just a few steps from the 18th green. And yet, it can feel like a whole different world. On the course, you're likely low on confidence and high on mistakes. Each swing reflects the self-doubt you hold deep inside. As the strokes add up, you sink further into existential misery.

In the clubhouse? It's a different story. As you trade heroic tales with other liars, your game transforms. You drive it like Rory McIlroy, hit your irons like vintage Tiger Woods, and scramble for par saves like Jordan Spieth. From the safety of the clubhouse, the only things more impressive than your golf game are your impeccable wardrobe and the car you parked in the lot.

There's just one problem with all of this bravado — everyone sees right through it. They're playing the same game, so they know it's all a lie. But they do it too. Round after round, golfers tell each other stories, each more exaggerated than the last. Eventually, the crowd breaks up, and everyone heads home. Until next week, when they return like clockwork, starting the whole strange ritual over again.

WHAT'S SAID vs. WHAT'S MEANT

Even in a golf clubhouse, where the insults flow freely, people sometimes hold back from saying what they really mean. Don't worry — we're here to help. You can use the list below as a translator, turning what someone said to you before or after a round into what they were really trying to say. Warning: feelings may be hurt.

"It took us a while to get through that round today."
You were lining up every putt like it was the last hole of the U.S. Open.

"Do you know who won our wagers?"
I know I did, and you better f*****g pay up.

"I think the clubhouse kitchen needs a couple more cooks."
Maybe you could get a job to pay off your lost bets.

"Have you found a partner for the next club tournament yet?"
Don't even think about asking me. There's no way I'm playing with you again.

"I can't believe how well you played today."
No, really. I can't believe it. You're usually so terrible.

"There are so many good golfers at this club."
I'm going to start playing with some of them instead of you.

"Thanks for buying the drinks."
The only thing higher than this bar tab is your score.

"What other hobbies do you have outside of golf?"
Start spending more time on those. You're wasting your time out here.

"I noticed you have a lot of nice clubs in the bag."
How much money did you waste on all that stuff?

"You sure you want to eat all that before we tee off?"
Better take an extra pair of trousers with you.

"Is there anyone around the clubhouse who could be our fourth?"
I'd love to play with at least one decent golfer today.

"Were you drinking on the course today?"

It sure looked like you were hammered.

"It's fun to watch golf on TV after our round."

Finally, golfers who know what they're doing.

"How long have you been playing golf?"

If I had to guess, I'd say about three days.

"Does your wife support your golf hobby?"

She's probably happy to just get rid of you for a few hours. I know the feeling.

"What's your favorite meal in the clubhouse restaurant?"

Probably the "Bogey Burrito", or perhaps the "Shank Tacos."

"This pro shop has some nice clubs."

You should buy some of them. Maybe you wouldn't suck so bad.

"Who's your favorite professional golfer?"
Your game reminds me of Phil Mickelson, only without all the talent.

"Do you think we could join this club?"
Well, I know I could, but I doubt they'd let you in.

"What are your goals for this golf season?"
Are you going to try to get worse? Lose more golf balls? Waste more time?

"I probably need to get going pretty soon."
It was bad enough spending four hours with you on the course. I don't need more in the clubhouse.

"I'd love to play this course more often."
As long as I don't have to play it with you.

"I'm going to head back out and play another nine holes."
Please don't come with me.

"Are you thinking about entering the club championship?"
You should think about entering rehab instead.

"Do you know many people at this club?"
I hope so, then I don't have to play with you all the time.

"You deserve to celebrate a good round with a cold drink."
That wasn't a good round, but I see you've got the drinking part down.

"How long did that round take us?"
It felt like years.

"Is it closing time already?"
Please, please tell me it's closing time. I can't take any more of this chatter.

"It was fun watching you play."
I take great pleasure in knowing I'm not the worst golfer at this club.

"You really hit some good shots today."
By "some," I mean a few. But you hit a ton of sh**y shots.*

FAMOUS GOLF FAILS

Golf is such a brutal game that even when the round is over — or before it's even begun — things can still go wrong. Not only are there plenty of famous golf fails that occurred between the 1st tee and the 18th green, but some also took place when the player wasn't even out on the course. You can take some twisted pleasure in reading the stories below and imagining the agony they caused.

Roberto De Vicenzo — 1968 Masters

When Roberto De Vicenzo walked off the 18th green on Sunday of the 1968 Masters, he believed that he had tied for the lead and would be facing Bob Goalby in a playoff the following day. Already the owner of an Open Championship title from 1967, this was another big step in the Argentine's career.

When he sat down in the clubhouse to sign his card and make it official, he didn't check the scores carefully. What should have been recorded as a "3" on the 17th hole was actually written down as a "4." That took De Vicenzo's score from a 65 to a 66. Once signed, the score could not be changed. He was now one stroke higher than Goalby, and the championship was over. Just like that, Bob Goalby was a Masters winner, and De Vicenzo had to live with an incredible mistake that had nothing to do with actually playing golf.

In addition to being a famous cautionary tale about checking your scorecard, this event also provided one of the great quotes in golf history. After learning of the mistake, De Vicenzo simply said, "What a stupid I am!"

Scottie Scheffler — 2024 PGA Championship

For professional golfers, there's a lot that goes into playing a major championship. They have to navigate big crowds just to get to the clubhouse before they can even start to prepare for the round. That's usually an uneventful process, but at the 2024 PGA Championship, it turned into anything but routine for the world's best player.

Scottie Scheffler was trying to get around traffic to enter the property and make it to the clubhouse. Accidentally, he went the wrong way, and a policeman took exception. Scheffler was removed from his car, arrested, and taken away from the course in the back of a cop car. The whole thing happened in the blink of an eye, and confusion reigned for the hours that followed.

Eventually, Scheffler was able to make it back to the course and managed to get ready in time to reach the first tee. While he didn't go on to win the event, his strange arrest will forever be remembered as one of the most unusual developments in golf.

Rory McIlroy — 2012 Ryder Cup

It's common for golfers to have trouble sleeping the night before a big event. The anticipation is strong, and most players just want to get to the course, spend some time in the clubhouse, and get started as soon as possible.

That wasn't the case for Rory McIlroy at the 2012 Ryder Cup. He overslept, having misunderstood his tee time due to a time zone mix-up. It took a police escort to get him to the course with just 10 minutes to spare before his tee time in the Sunday singles. Without any time to warm up, he scrambled to the tee and faced off against Keegan Bradley.

Did McIlroy struggle all day after such a ragged start? Not so much. He beat Bradley 2&1, and Team Europe pulled off a stunning comeback that's now known as the Miracle at Medinah. To add to the legend of this fateful day, one of the PGA employees who helped McIlroy scramble to make it to the event was a young woman who would later become his wife. Without a doubt, this turned out to be one of the best cases of oversleeping in sports history.

WEIRD GOLF RULES

Did you know that the rules of golf can still get you when you aren't even playing a round? This is especially true if you're participating in a competition. The rules below are yet another example of how golf's rules are always looking for every possible opportunity to completely ruin your day.

- **You can't practice on the course before a round.**
  If you venture out onto the course to practice before your round actually begins, you could add penalty strokes to your score before you even hit your first official shot. What a sh***y way to start your day!

- **Being late can cost you strokes — or more.**
  Did the clubhouse take a bit longer than expected to prepare your food? Tough luck. You can be assessed a two-stroke penalty if you're late to the tee in a competition, and if you're too late, you could be disqualified entirely.

- **Signing an incorrect scorecard is a big problem.**
  For some reason, if you sign for the wrong score, you can't just fix the mistake later. Signing for a higher score means you're stuck with that higher score, while signing for a lower score could get you disqualified from the tournament entirely.

CONCLUSION:
SEE YOU NEXT ROUND

If you've made it to the end of this book, congratulations — you now have a new, brutally honest understanding of this ridiculous game we all love to hate: golf.

So, are you ready to quit and take up a sport that makes a little more sense? Maybe something where the people you play with don't spend four hours lying to your face? Something where you might actually have a bit of skill?

Nah, not a chance. This is your game — our game — and quitting is just not an option. We should, without a doubt, but we won't.

Golf is like life in so many ways. It's easy to get fed up, frustrated, and ready to throw in the towel. But the next day, we get up, brush ourselves off, and give it another shot.

Golf is no different. After a rough round — or maybe a whole string of them — you'll swear you're done for good. But then, out of nowhere, you'll catch that sweet spot on the clubface.

How? Who knows. You made the same messed-up swing you always do, but this time it lands just right. The ball takes off, holds its line, and lands perfectly by the target. For once, your buddies are genuinely impressed. They don't even have to lie when they say, "Nice shot."

Just like that, you're back in. All in.

Suddenly, you're thinking about new clubs, new courses, maybe even signing up for the Club Championship — foolishly convinced that maybe, just maybe, you've cracked the code.

You haven't. Of course you haven't. But that doesn't matter.

Because in golf, logic doesn't apply. One great shot erases 94 disasters. One birdie forgives a front-nine apocalypse. And one good round? That'll keep your delusions alive for months.

And to wrap this up in true golf fashion, here's one last message — absolutely, totally, and definitely not a lie:

You're a great golfer with a bright future ahead on the course. We believe in you.

(Just don't check your scorecard.)

BEMBERTON
BOOKS

ENJOY THE LAUGHS?

If this book gave you a chuckle, made you snort into your coffee, or reminded you of that one friend—I'd love it if you could leave a quick review or a star rating on Amazon.

(Seriously, it takes less time than lining up a three-foot putt.)

Your review helps other golfers find this book and feel slightly better about their own performance. Thanks a million!

To leave a review & help spread the word

SCAN HERE